I CAN SIGN MY A B Cs

Susan Gibbons Chaplin
Illustrated by Laura McCaul

KENDALL GREEN PUBLICATIONS
Gallaudet University Press
Washington, D.C.

Kendall Green Publications
An imprint of Gallaudet University Press
Washington, DC 20002

Published 1986. 10 09 08 07 06 05 04 03 02   13 12 11 10 9 8 7 6 5
Printed in Korea

Library of Congress Cataloging-in-Publication Data

Chaplin, Susan Gibbons, 1956-
   I can sign my ABCs.

   Summary: An introduction to the alphabet in sign language with the manual alphabet handshape, a picture,
the name, and the sign of an object beginning with that letter for each of the twenty-six letters of the alphabet.
   1. Sign language–Juvenile literature. 2. Alphabet–Juvenile literature. [1. Sign language. 2. Alphabet]
I. McCaul, Laura, ill. II. Title.
HV2476.C46 1986   419'.03'21 [E]   86-22890

ISBN 0-930323-19-X

To Lindsey, David, and Madeline

Aa

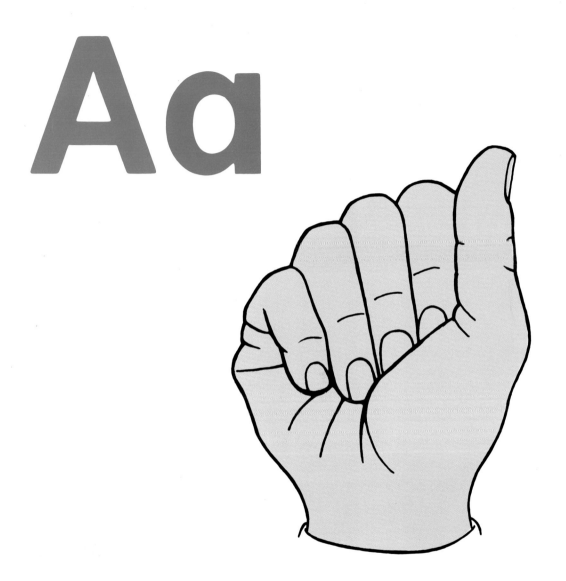

a b c d e f g h i j k l m n o p q r s t u v w x y z

apple

B b

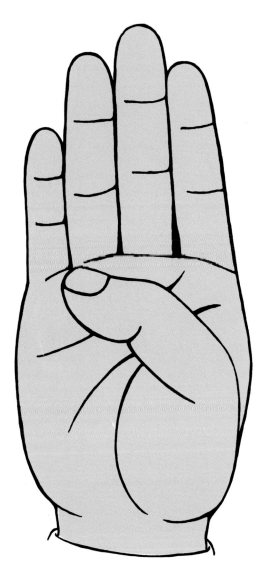

a b c d e f g h i j k l m n o p q r s t u v w x y z

ball

Cc

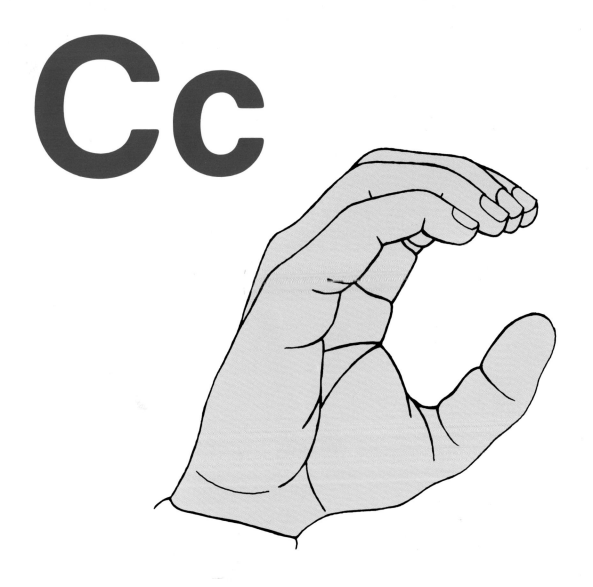

a b c d e f g h i j k l m n o p q r s t u v w x y z

cat

Dd

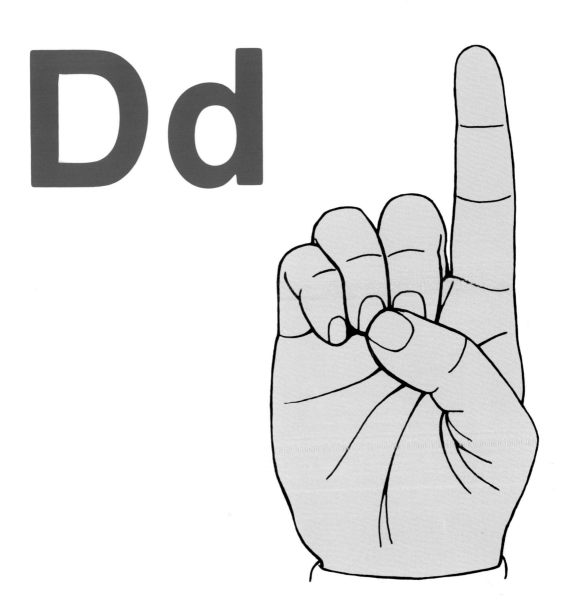

abcdefghijklmnopqrstuvwxyz

E e

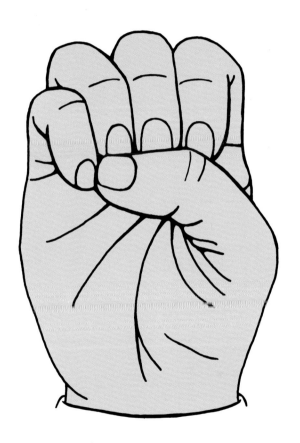

abcd**e**fghijklmnopqrstuvwxyz

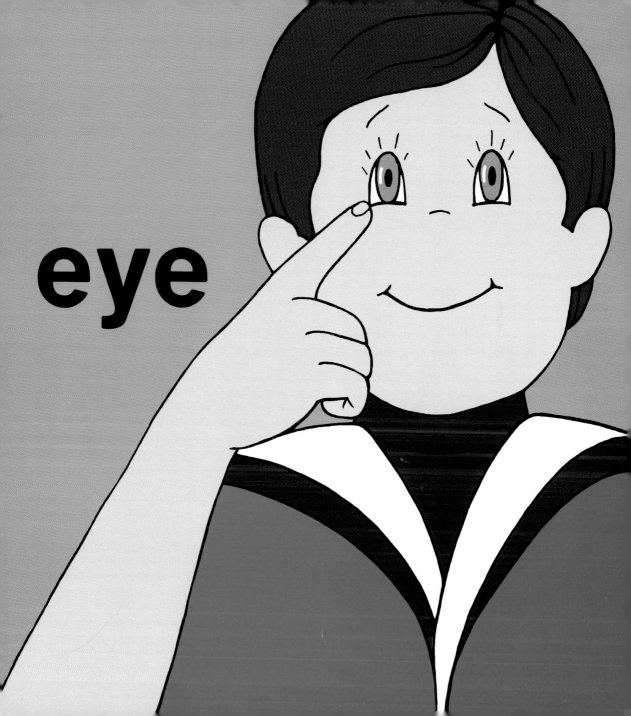

eye

Ff

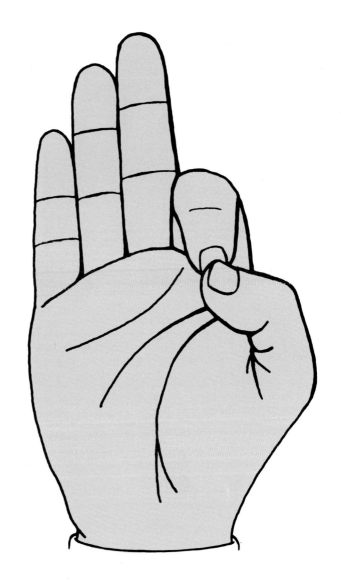

abcde**f**ghijklmnopqrstuvwxyz

flower

Gg

abcdef**g**hijklmnopqrstuvwxyz

glass

Hh

abcdefg**h**ijklmnopqrstuvwxyz

hat

Ii

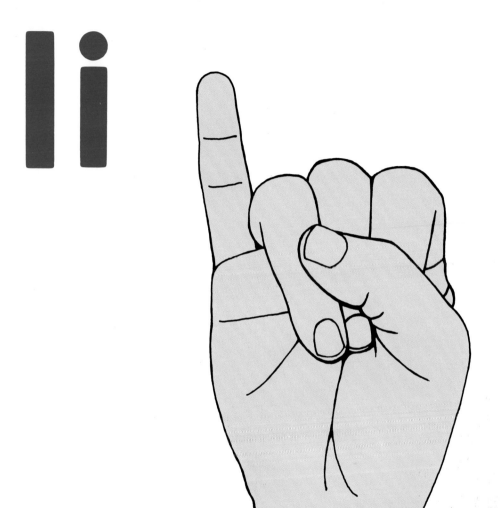

abcdefgh**i**jklmnopqrstuvwxyz

ice
cream

Jj

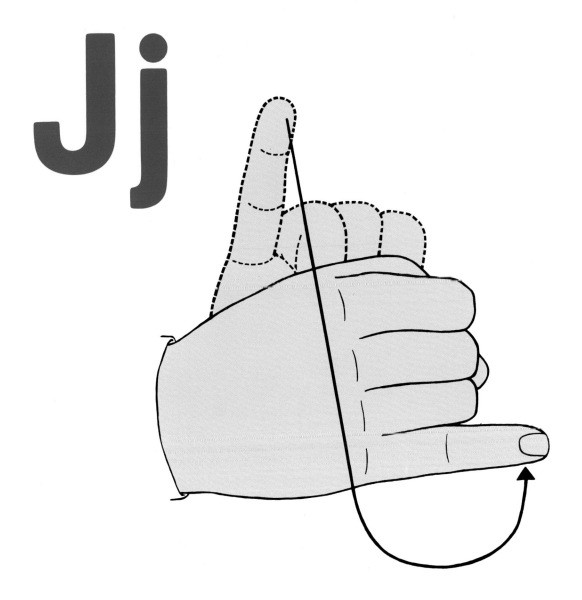

abcdefghijklmnopqrstuvwxyz

Kk

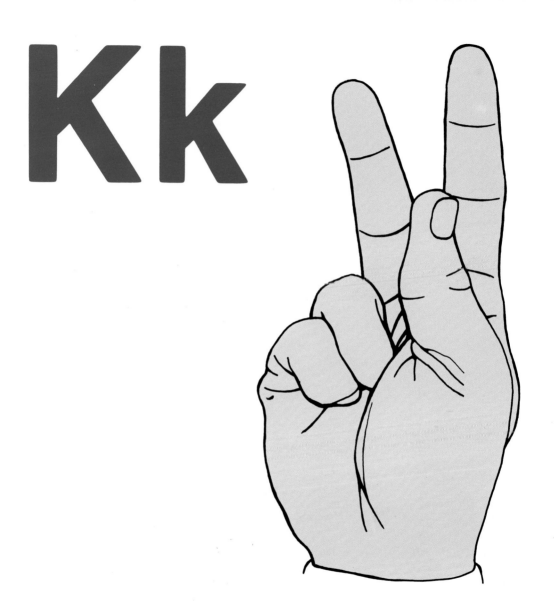

abcdefghij**k**lmnopqrstuvwxyz

key

Ll

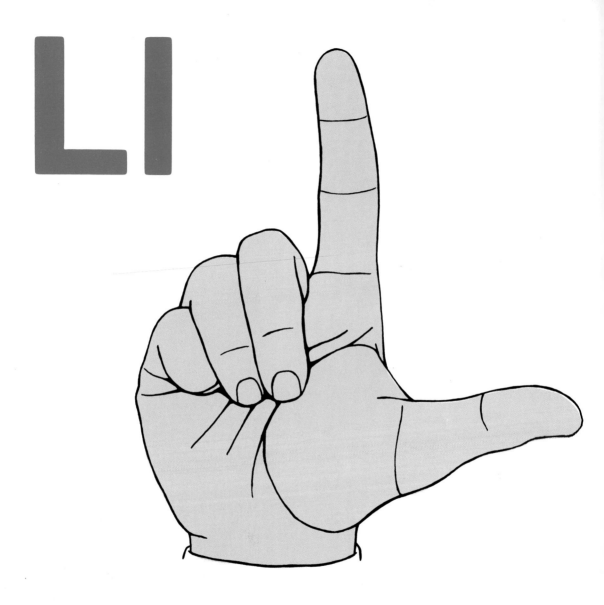

abcdefghijk**l**mnopqrstuvwxyz

light

Mm

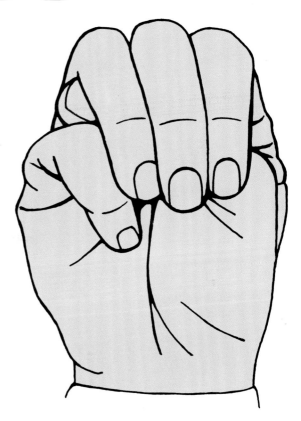

abcdefghijkl m nopqrstuvwxyz

milk

Nn

abcdefghijklm**n**opqrstuvwxyz

nose

Oo

abcdefghi j klmn**o**pqrstuvwxyz

orange

Pp

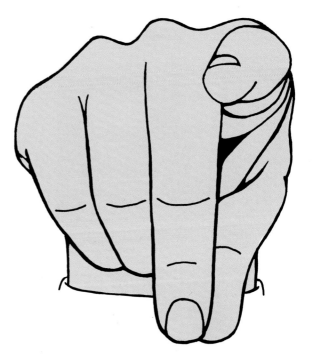

abcdefghijklmno**p**qrstuvwxyz

pig

Qq

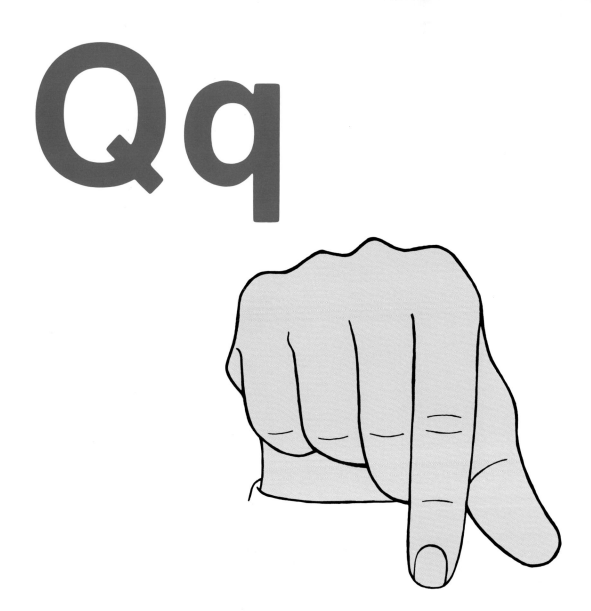

abcdefghijklmnop**q**rstuvwxyz

queen

Rr

abcdefghijklmno p q **r** s t u v w x y z

rabbit

Ss

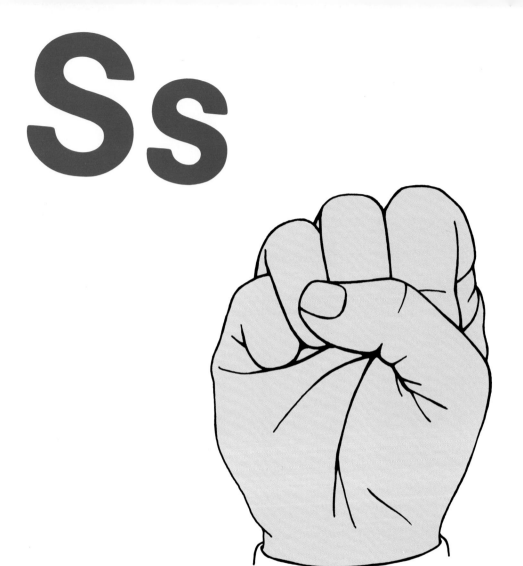

abcdefghijklmnopqr**s**tuvwxyz

shoes

Tt

abcdefghijklmnopqrs**t**uvwxyz

tree

Uu

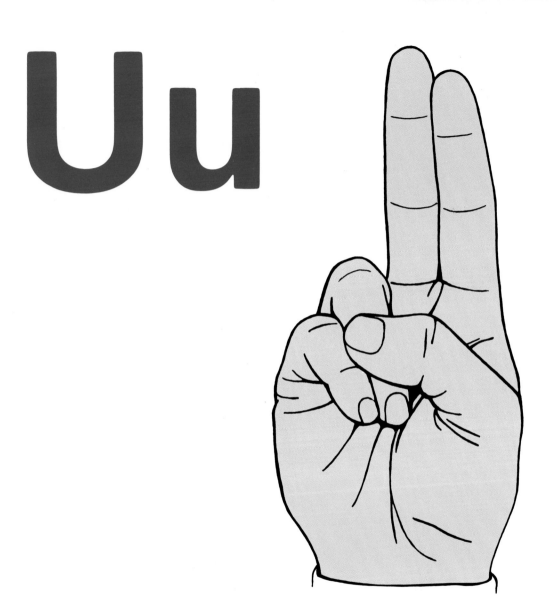

abcdefghijklmnopqrstuvwxyz

umbrella

Vv

abcdefghijklmnopqrstu**v**wxyz

valentine

W w

abcdefghijklmnopqrstu**vw**xyz

window

X x

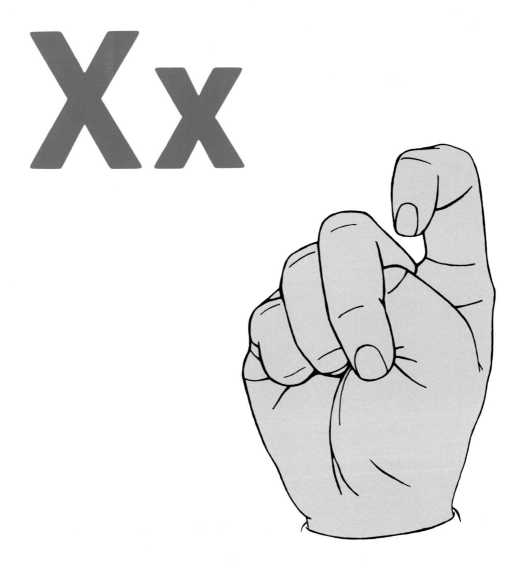

abcdefghijklmnopqrstuvw**x**yz

xylophone

Yy

abcdefghijklmnopqrstuvwx**y**z

yo-yo

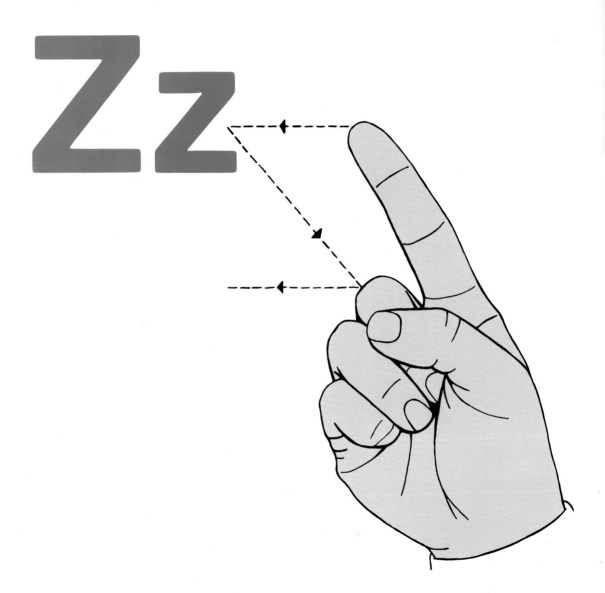

abcdefghijklmnopqrstuvwxyz

zipper